SLOW LORIS POETRY SERIES

GREEN IN THE BODY

GREEN IN THE BODY

Robert Winner

SLOW LORIS PRESS
Pittsburgh

A number of these poems were first published in *American Poetry Review*, *Trans-Atlantic Review*, *New Letters*, *Confrontation*, *Westigan Review*, and *Ontario Review*.

The poem "The Banjo" appeared originally in *The New Yorker*.

Printed in the United States of America
Hoechstetter Printing Company
Pittsburgh, Pennsylvania

First Printing, January 1979

Library of Congress Cataloging in Publication Data
Winner, Robert, 1930-
    Green in the body.

(Slow Loris Poetry Series)
I. Title. II. Series
PS3573.I5323C7 811'.5'4   78-27912
ISBN 0-918366-15-1
ISBN 0-918366-14-3 pbk.

SLOW LORIS PRESS
923 Highview Street
Pittsburgh, Pennsylvania 15206

for Sylvia

CONTENTS

THE SANITY OF EARTH AND GRASS

AMONG THESE ROCKS

UNPREDICTABLE ROADS

Ah! Douce campagna, honey in the heart
Green in the body, out of a petty phrase,
Out of a thing believed, a thing affirmed . . .
                              Wallace Stevens

THE SANITY OF EARTH AND GRASS

HORSES

I look across some ragged meadows
where I played in summers years before.
Over the neighbor's fence, three horses—
two chestnuts and a dappled gray.
They have been free all night
without a scrap of leather on them,
grazing, huddling close, or moving lazily about.
They seem to have the world to themselves.

I stay there watching them, as if I could eat grass.
The trees are working, they work like stones,
and the horses are a game of childhood,
they are half-ton butterflies.
This meadow is the universe
and I could walk and walk and never reach those horses
always before my eyes the smile of their glossy coats
in the summer sun, the thick grass wet and ripe.

I have walked in the wrong direction all my life,
balancing on railroad tracks away
from anything I could love as well
as that supple ground, that tangled knee-deep grass,
those horses waiting in the expectant distance
watching me come with my wet knees pocked with burrs,
my bridles and my daylight mysteries,
to place my hands against their springy necks,
to feel their strange obedience,
and take my boyhood in my hands again.

THE CHAIN GANG

Stripped to the waist,
hard-muscled, downcast, under the guns
of lounging guards, they are clearing a roadside
across a palmetto landscape.

I notice one blond boy swinging a pick,
broad-shouldered. His skin is smooth, bright, sweaty.
His upright body ripples
under the rigid fury of his face.

His bulging eyes fixed on the ground
can see mountains, the destiny
of his imagination he can never get to,
where he could rest, a lion
in the wilderness of his flesh.

I see the body with its own career of gestures—
its bright roads, its dark roads
apart, serene . . .

Men must be carved, apparently,
like slaughtered steers or pigs
to find the marble of their bones
innocent,
innocent after all
as the stones they break, or rain,
or the guards in cages of their white voices

Trapped in one chained line,
one terrifying combination of arrangements,
driven to taste each other's flesh . . .

The body sings alone

among the earth's arrangements
ignorant of crimes or dreams
or the curious idea of justice.

BUZZARD

In a roofless quiet,
floating on bits of wind,
its great flat wings
thrust out
from its entrails.

To fly is lovely . . .
it is the prince of ugliness,
its crooked head points down,
a finger carving toneless rings
in a blue eye-world.

DESERTED FARM

The broken walls remain,
smothered by scrawled weeds,
sumac, prodigal flights of vines
over stones and windows.

I press my fingers down
on grass that was once
part of a dooryard,
or someone's shadow,
and feel it tremble,
escape.

For the grass might be any one, a boy
who felt the first touch of desire
and turned away.

GOLDENROD

I meet in the morning
the dauntless spinster, quick-smiled,
leather-skinned, flat-shoed,
and friendly as the tree her dog waters.

Always cheerful to me and strangers
I don't know her kitchen mind
her closet mood
her cornered evenings facing darkness.

She comes from the country where goldenrod
commandeers meadows in September,
hailing its own tall yellow over the spent grass,
spilling its pollen like sunlight—
and who cares which of the bright tough flowers
breeds the field again.

20

SPRING

Laughter leaps up out of the dead park,
an old black woman's laughter
bearing the dawn of trees
the unexpected self.

EDEN

The earth has never needed us.
At an abandoned railway station
small bleached buildings
kneel before the sun. Serene,
they have no more battles to fight
against light and cold.

All the sadness of walls forgotten—
drifting back to earth, disengaged
from the triumph of billboards and schedules,
the rushing arroyos of sweat,
the cracking bones against starvation.
Weeds bury the rails'
four rusty teeth laid out
along the river's mercury slab.

High in their winds, the hoodlum gulls
glide down to sunlit water, like ideas
descending to reality. In mounds of leaves
squirrels and mice forage
in their morose routines, all of them
breathing a cry of life
with the whole world Sunday—
an everyday like the animals' hunger.

9 TO 5

How can the wind find me—
on this street, caught between
disciplined walls of office buildings,
windows of fish silence,
stratagems of hunger behind glass?

How can it slam against my body,
tear around me, surprise me—
diving among walls to touch my face—
bearing its dust, its swill-thick river smells—
surround me with the forest's privacy,
the sanity of earth and grass,
the sea stretched out beside this island
like the fin of sleep?

TO MY FACE, AFTER ILLNESS

From your bones on out
you give the lie to suffering.
You ought to be more lined with pain.
You should make a stronger impression
in photographs
of the heartbreak caged in your fat.

Mess of tissues!
Maybe I should be grateful to you
for remembering,
for leaving printed on this flesh—
its sun-tanned jowls—
those inescapable paragraphs
which tell the original story.

STONE IN AUGUST

Sun-whitened, sprawled in deep grass,
small reflections laced with quartz and iron,
a continent's milk compressed.

Sweet ship of summer floating in the field
all banners blowing in the heat burned into you
plunged in some vital silence of your own
that even to the wind is central.

Quietness made before mind, sustained,
the years flow into you and you hold them
without decay, bone of the intangible

Red of fish and vulture's white
snake's blue and the clouds—
the summer's gladness of your being
heaved from the earth,

I would dance on you, stone.
I would make more life of you.

A WAR

The green marsh wakens with birds at dusk
from the afternoon sleep of cattails—
sandpipers wading on thin bent legs,
sparrows clinging to reeds,
and herons stalking somewhere in small channels.

It gives me joy to know them, near
to my great walks out of boyhood, to feel
the rancid breath of wilderness touch my face
the stride in front of me,
the world in front of my shoes.

Just behind me, the highway. Traffic, blazing
islands of gas pumps, fast-food joints—
a screen of light against the darkening sky.

I watch some killdeer peck at the rubbled margins,
tasting our swill in their swamp food.
They hop among three yellow bulldozers
parked haphazardly for the night.
How strange and brave they are to come,
fighting for their small lives almost in secret.

PENGUINS

In the long months between nestings
in the fierce Antarctica,
no one has ever found them.
They disappear as we do under faces and clothes.
I laugh at the way they stand up straight,
at the flapping of their atrophied wings.
I have seen one die in a seal's mouth—
ripped to skeleton and beak and floating blood
in a matter of thirty seconds.

THE LOOK OF THINGS

I gaze at the mountains—their green
the green of my strength,
their white my spirit's white, reaching
from death to the clarity of morning.

This is the dialogue I want:
language that answers itself—
as with the sky, to behold
and to be beheld.

AMONG THESE ROCKS

A MESSAGE FROM MY UNCLE FELIX, A
HUNCHBACK, PASSING AN APARTMENT
HOUSE IN GREENWICH VILLAGE WHERE HE
LIVED IN THE NINETEEN THIRTIES

I strain along the sidewalk, dragging myself
from the hole of the subway
to the hole of my house.

These firemen lounging
in the open doors of the firehouse
gauge me with their careful distant eyes
like a collapse in a blazing house.

They do not know that I am one with them
in my vanity, longing upward
toward ladders and exploits.

I am for them the dense improbable horror
they can never quite believe in—
their secret deformity, their
monster from a fairy tale.

Here on this street—
a splash of night clubs, gift shops, sex shops,
sausage and pizza vendors, restaurants and bars—
all the equipment of pleasure—
this street where, forty years ago, I lived
under the shadow scars of elevated tracks—
what has it got to show for happiness,
this street of the young and the washed up?

A crazy sadness drags its eyes
in the pavement's filth.
I'm surprised to see two lovers

31

meet on the corner,
their arms around each other,
unabashed as actors.

LATE NOVEMBER WOODS

The trees give off a dangerous silence.
In solitude. Exposed. Confronting winter.
The sun sinks. The cold
drives deeper into the air, like a nail.

I am out of all the world's doors.
The blue jays rifle past; they are at home here,
in charge of things.
My life seems counterfeit, a forged check.

Back in my car again, I drive with relief
to the city's glass, street hustlers and
smoldering gypsy warmth.
I'm wrapped in the enamelled confidence
of a crowd. I mingle comfortably,
braced in my con man's smile.

ON LEXINGTON AVENUE

What I like is smell,
the deep beef smell of broiling hamburger
taking over the street,
spreading its animal strength within
this tunnel of stinging gasoline.

It knocks me off the long day's pedestal
of abstraction—odorless
daydreams in offices—

To teach me again
the enormous kindness of sensation—
for after all what is
the smell of a good intention
or of grief?

THE SHIRT

The freshness of my shirt this morning
straightens me up:
its urbane gloss and pride
a fabric of myself,
another identity pulled from a sleeve.

Appearances waken me:
a cool sun slides on the plaster walls;
the windows open on trees,
men moving in the street to work;
clouds bloom in the marble distance.
The sky without an identity bursts upward.

We stumble through common dreams,
defended in these walls,
hidden in light and light,
the mystery of surfaces
opening like the sea's silk
fresh beginnings in which I dress myself.

THE BANJO

There is some demon turning me into an old man,
living like a tapeworm in my gut,
turning me into a snowman
of cleaned up fingernails and shaving cream,
while somewhere in the life I forgot to live
an old rapscallion banjo sleeps with dust.

I'd like to take that banjo to my job
and sit cross-legged, strum and strum
and wake those rigid people into dancing—
those white men so white their smiles are water,
those camouflaged men who cruise
around each other like soft battleships.

I'd like them to remember their bare feet,
the bite of dust and sun down country roads,
the face they forgot to desire
carved and wrinkled as a peach pit . . .

All of them nailed to their careers
like handles on boxes!
There is some other game for me,
another reality could walk in any time
and become the boss,
shouting Dance! Dance! Dance!
Dance through partitions!
Dance through stairwells, envelopes, telephones!

It's hard to know which life is sleep
or where the door is with my real name on it.

A SEPIA PHOTOGRAPH OF MY GRANDFATHER

He's sitting on cushions in the middle of Asia
wearing a turban, a hookah near him
and a scimitar.
               From Lodz, a textile merchant,
he travelled like a Phoenician,
buying cotton in Bokhara, Galveston, or Egypt.

It seems miraculous how they went everywhere
like English milords—these Jews
walking the thinnest silver line
of toleration.
               To escape the pogroms,
he sold his factory and his house
and skipped across the border with his family—
from Poland to Germany—my mother
hidden once in a clothes trunk—
and then to England, where his business failed,
at last America, where—
used up, penniless—he died.

Here, in this faded card, he's young:
he's playing out the charade of his adventure—
that short half-century of freedom
between ghetto and holocaust.
As if he knew it would end in human smoke
he took, reluctantly, that wandering step
to find another country, another street
where they could put their bundles down,
light candles, bake their bread
and spread the cloth for their festivals.

IN 1938

Bickerstaff ate the school's free lunch:
watery soup with carrots, white bread,
apple, half-pint bottle of milk.
Public food on greasy trays
he ate in silence.

Charity that he had to take
like a badly fitting sweater.
It belonged to his Bickerstaff being—
thin-boned, sallow, dust-poor.

I remember him among weedy alleys
and secretive wooden houses,
hair so blond it was almost the color of light
above the pointed bones of his face.
In worn-out corduroy knickers
and hopeless sneakers
he walked the broken pavements of our street.

CHALK

Below the fire escapes
the boy with the cracked skull
spreads like a flower.

Were we happy then? Were we happy,
ballplayers in the hospital anteroom
staring as a coffin black as curbstones
drags up the last sudden love
of the stranger father
flinging his body over it?

Later, I bend my head
near his house, thinking—
the body is rotting now
beneath sunlight—It's still morning?—
The chalk-marked pavement waits
for the game to resume.

TUGBOAT

Bright on the dark
drifting ashes of January . . .
head lifted back,
a fist of diesel confidence . . .
spray slung up, snubbed bow
slamming the waves, the icy slack
at the river's mouth,

your power grows
around a crazy idea of its own
unruly possibilities in the
careening water, you
with your heart of flame, your energy
like a belief in yourself.

WINTER LOAFING

I leave work early, out of step
with the rhythm of these office buildings
gathering steam until they could burst,
their glass hands clapping against the sky.

I drift downstairs with the snow.
Outside, the trees uphold the rhythm
of space and seasons—
black indications of long rests
in a movement of silence. The lights go on
as secretively as the tuning of a harp.

I guess I'm afraid of my death,
of missing out,
of never being able to taste the fruit of idleness,
and so I stand on corners, stand and look
that the day may not die,
and see the people pour from the office buildings
in a dark bright stream,
and the sun
like an old man's pink face, like a rose among graves.

UNPREDICTABLE ROADS

SOUSA

I like John Philip Sousa.
His face is shiny and creased
like his bandmaster's uniform.
They have walked on his mind
in a hundred thousand parades.
He never takes it personally.

He tells them where to go:
the bugles, the needling flutes, and drums
pounding against the noon of clarinets,
trombones that bray the pleasures
of war—those thrills

of a past you joyously invent,
funny music, finding its struts and swaggers
in our goose-stepping bloodstreams,
the enemy always with tricky eyes,
downright wrongheadedness and make believe teeth.

Tell them where to get off
John Philip Sousa
forever and ever.

JOB

Who knows what this One will be up to next?
Better to wait quiet and patient
while He drowns three schoolboys in a sailboat,
sets fire to a row of tenements,
and pushes clouds beyond a dying farm.

Actually I would like to groan and weep and understand this fellow
but even a sob sounds like laughter to Him
for He thinks He's only playing
and like a drunk at a party
He likes everyone.

BOYS PLAYING FRISBEE

You know the obedience
of your body like a lover.
Nothing you do makes a fool of you.
The disk lets you do anything—
it floats—
it dreams in the wind.

Like a lizard's tongue, you snap it
from the golden air.
You laugh with your wrists.
You shine.
You dare to glide through unfamiliar dances,
and move as only the best can,
only the naturals.

ELEGY

I remember the feel of a hammer—
its grainy handle placing
its head's steel weight in your palm,
or the rung of a ladder
pressing confidently into your foot,
or how the sun felt on your skin, or cold water
as it dissolved the wall of salt
at the back of your throat.

I remember how you sang in your stone shoes
light-voiced as dusk or feathers,
how your shoes turned outward again—
as they used to when you walked—
when you lay in your dead body on the floor
and showed us the shining nail-heads
around each earth-scuffed leather sole.

MISS ALDERMAN

By the high steel hospital bed
a thousand miles from anyone I knew,
she sat while I slept:
Miss Alderman, night duty student nurse
with auburn hair, blue eyes, a perfect body.

Sixteen, just inside girl hunger,
paralyzed, sleeping on my side,
I dreamt of her in my fever,
my spine like a broken chair
on one of their broken Southern porches.

Coming out of sick half-sleep, I found her
pressing my face with her parted lips.
Desire leaped in me, all my body
helpless to respond like a sack of gravel.
I could see her breast.
A warm deep wave of her carried me off.
She kissed me, fondled me; she cared enough
to want to give me
some of that which haunts me,
heals me, makes things right.

It haunts me now that only chance with her,
that tenderness
lost to me in some provincial Southern city,
a nurse still maybe, or a housewife.

I knew it was no more
than kindness
by the blank calm way
she fixed her hair at the mirror

and scraped her lipstick
with her fingernail
and buttoned her dress
afterwards.

THE NIGHT

In pain, the body
turns without memories,
grieving in darkness
at the perfect designs
of organs, like stars—
impenitent, unstained—
until the mind is caught,
must turn to meet a stranger's
bloodshot eyes and grinning gums,
and swim with him
in a perversion that is itself
both love
and the sun darkened with waste.

THE YOUTH GHOST

Glimpsed at the ends of vaguely familiar
streets, he resembles me, I catch him
loitering in crowds that seem
to possess him, push him under their flow—
he flashes out of it,
nimbly keeping himself intact.

Coming on him quickly, I'm startled
seeing his pants too short, his hat
that doesn't come all the way down—
all his clothes worn-out,
his eyes inhabiting dream landscapes;
detailed adventures on maps without night.

He goes without speaking, leaving me
amazed he could survive so well without me,
thriving in refusal to release himself
from books, fields, pavements,
or the melody of houses where I left him,
or occupied with climbing trees and laughter,
the smells of gasoline and barns,
and the long inviting unpredictable roads.

LEARNING TO MOURN

I'm an inexperienced mourner,
I don't even know how to begin
to cry out like that old man
wailing in the next ward—
oi weih, oi weih—his two sounds
beating like a head against the wall.

He makes me squirm
but I get his message better than my own.
How can I free myself like him?
How can I know my place as he does,
know how little I am?
How can I mourn, cry out violent sorrow
like the cheep of a trapped bird?

Old man, teach me.
Help me to reach the bowels of my cry
and bring it up, coarse, rasping.
Teach me to be disgusting.
Help me to exile myself from all
the populations of eyes and ears.
Teach me to live in that country
where no one else is, where I can
bash to pieces with my howl
good breeding, priests and pillars.
Let my heart shake. Let me feel just once
what you do—with no one else there
and no illusions, the *self* wiped out,
unable to see or hear or understand.

Old man, you are senseless, stupid, repulsive,
lying in your shit. I love your mourning.
You've let the angel of death from your mouth.
I hear one minute of your unforgiving protest

53

that is like true song: reckless, fatal singing,
song that is not victorious for once,
not even consoling,
merely a sound you have to make.

IN A CHURCHYARD

I study moss-green tilted gravestones.
I finger their names, dates and worn words
and watch them pace through time, like clouds,
when, miles away, they find my father

dead on the bathroom floor.
My wife blows her breath into his blue mouth,
she pounds his chest . . .

Where was I then?—so out of it, miles
away, so out of it, like a fussy rector
dabbling with gravestones.
They seemed to skip like flies between generations.

Robert Winner was born in New York City in 1930 and has lived there ever since. He worked as a stockbroker for nineteen years and recently became president of a small company in suburban New Jersey. He has studied with Galway Kinnell and David Ignatow.

Green in the Body, in the Slow Loris Press series of books, has been published by Anthony and Patricia Petrosky on January 1, 1979. Publication of this book was made possible by a grant from the National Endowment for the Arts.